The Little Book of
of
CYNICS

Crombie Jardine
PUBLISHING LIMITED
Office 2
3 Edgar Buildings
George Street
Bath
BA1 2FJ

www.crombiejardine.com

This edition was first published by
Crombie Jardine Publishing Limited in 2007

ISBN 978-1-906051-00-6

Written by Derek Thompson and David French

Typesetting and cover design
by Ben Ottridge

Printed and bound in Great Britain by William Clowes Ltd, Beccles, Suffolk

Contents

INTRODUCTION

Cynics are as old as Man himself. Ancient sources tell of Adam who, when seeing Eve for the first time, muttered, "Uh-oh. There goes Free Will." If Adam was indeed the father of the human race – and, as such, the progenitor of cynicism – is it any surprise his children are just like him?

In fact, it was Antisthenes, a follower of Socrates, who got the ball officially rolling. The original philosopher Cynic sought happiness through virtue, rejecting the obsessions of the time: pleasure, fame, fortune and power. Antisthenes, it's said, once declared, "I would rather go mad than experience pleasure" – not someone you'd want on your list of wedding guests.

Nowadays, the word 'cynic' has been relegated to a synonym of 'doubter', 'pessimist' or 'sceptic'. But, given our modern preoccupations with pleasure, fame, fortune and power, maybe we need cynics more than ever. Perhaps theirs is that small, sane voice amid the roar of instant gratification, 24-hour television, media manipulation and marketing.

Or perhaps we just wanted to sell a book. But, of course – we're not that cynical. Are we?

APHORISMS

He who laughs
last will probably
be laughed at next.

A fool and his
money are a joy
to behold.

A thing of beauty
is a marketing
opportunity.

Two heads are
better than one,
but it's hard to
find a hat that fits.

When the pupil
is ready the guru
will rip him off.

Never look a
gift-horse in the
mouth while
it exhales.

In the kingdom
of the bland the
one-idea-ed man
is king.

The journey of
a thousand miles
begins on the
wrong airplane.

The fruit of
success is rooted
in the manure
of publicity.

Mosquito is deadly
but flea's a jolly
good fellow.

A middle-aged man and his hair are soon parted.

The early bird is probably hungry.

The wages of sin are tax-free.

When one door
closes another
trap-door opens.

A horse may
be capable of great
generosity, but an
oyster will only
ever be shellfish.

Happy is the man that findeth wisdom, for the cheap merchandise thereof contains the quality of gold.

Blessed are the
meek, for they
expect little and
get little.

People who live
in glass houses
shouldn't expect to
be cool in summer
and warm in winter.

People who live
in glass houses – do
they have windows?

Send a fool to market and he'll sell himself.

Not only is money the root of all evil, it's a proven cause of smugness.

Life is short, art is long, and opera is interminable.

It is easier for
a camel to pass
through the eye of
a needle than for a
rich man to submit
his tax-returns
honestly.

Not even faith can move EU Common Agricultural Policy food mountains.

Judge a businessman by the companies he keeps bankrupting.

One man's meat is another man's E.coli infection.

That which does
not kill me only
damages me
irreparably.

A friend in need
is a burden.

As soon as he is
born man begins
to die. For relief,
man in his wisdom
invented taxes.

Appearances can be
completely accurate.

As you sow, so shall you develop backache.

Great leaders are borne.

Factions speak louder than herds.

Marriage – proof that prison doesn't work.

Life is a series of ups and downs. Today, you're in despair, but tomorrow you'll be restored to misery again.

It's always darkest just before it goes pitch black.

Don't put all your eggs in one fertility clinic.

One man's loss
is another man's
pension shortfall.

What some call
safety in numbers
accountants call
cooking the books.

A patient friend
loveth at all times,
but phoning at 3am
is plain stupid.

There is a way that
seemeth right unto a
man, but a woman
shall always find
something wrong
with it.

Nothing is
more stupid than
striking a man –
especially a man
who strikes back.

Where there are prawns there are probably crackers.

Before Enlighten-
ment, chop wood;
after Enlightenment,
install central
heating.

Where two
fat people are
gathered a third
shall find his
path blocked.

Children should
be seen and not
hoodies.

Man that is born of
Jewish woman has
but few years if he
forgets her birthday.

Behind every
successful marriage
is a mistress trying
to get out.

Behind every
Caesar is a Brutus.

Cast thy nets
upon the waters
and thou shalt
deplete fish stocks.

All the world's a
stage and everyone
thinks he's the
producer.

He who lives by
the sword shall
probably die a
cliché.

Better late than
dead.

Happy the bride
who comes to her
senses before the
ceremony ends.

It's always darkest
just before dawn.
But then it rains all
day and your roof
blows off. Then it
gets dark again.

The way to a man's heart attack is a full-fat diet.

There's no such thing as misogyny: there's just oestrogen intolerance.

Rejection – it's just life's way of telling you you're not wanted.

Swimming – not only a great way to keep fit but a wonderful opportunity to urinate in a public place.

Walking – the perfect way to give your arse a rest.

In life, there are the 'cans' and the 'can'ts'. Most people are a bit of a can't.

German philosophy is a Nietzsche market.

Too many cooks spoil the TV schedule.

Many vans make
light removal
work.

A rolling stone
refuses to stop
touring.

A splash in the pan is worth two damp patches on the floor.

An apple a day keeps the doctor idle on a £250,000 a year salary.

All good things
must come to an
end before 1am
(according to the
Environmental
Health Authority).

Bovinism – the last refuge of the cow.

Man cannot live by bread alone, especially if he's gluten-intolerant.

Celebrities – living proof that evolution can take a wrong turn.

Farming makes a man sensitive to the wondrous cycles of Nature. Plus, it beats starving.

School holidays – the happiest days of your teachers' lives.

Out of the
mouths of babes
and sucklings comes
green puke.

To an English
batsman there is no
rest for the wicket.

It is better to give
violent blows than
to receive.

Beauty is only
as deep as your
finances will
afford cosmetic
dermatology.

A lie for a lie, a
truth for a truth.

A bimbo's eyes are
the glazed windows
of her soul.

Better to have love and lust than never to have lust at all.

QUESTIONS

Which sandwich came first – the chicken or the egg?

Why do internationally famous clairvoyants need to advertise?

Self-help groups – aren't they a contradiction in terms?

If Mithras is Roman, Jehovah is Jewish and Minerva is Greek, what exactly <u>is</u> the language of the Gods?

When human beings were given Free Will did they have a choice in the matter?

If meat is murder, aren't vegetables manslaughter?

Who needs Free Will when we have the government to decide for us?

If a debit card takes money out of your account shouldn't a credit card put money in?

When they experiment on animals why don't they try experimenting with compassion?

If coffee is considered a cash crop why do farmers get the least cash from it?

Why ban smokers
from public places
when you can have
much more fun
by banning them
from breathing
out?

Why aren't chips
served in vegetarian
restaurants?

If the best things
in life are free why
are luxury goods
so expensive?

If no man is an
island then what
exactly is the Isle
of Man?

Why are there
no new Chinese
proverbs?

How can there
be a world-wide
conspiracy if people
already suspect?

If dolphins are
so intelligent how
come they can't
ride a bicycle?

What would happen if a vampire bit a werewolf and vice-versa?

Why <u>are</u> cheap things cheerful?

If chocolate is
better than sex
why do the stains
look more suspect?

If time is a
relative concept,
does this explain
all-day breakfasts?

INSTRUCTIONS AND PRECEPTS

Support international charities. For it is written – the begging-bowl of thy neighbour will look good in an art gallery.

Do unto others while their backs are turned.

Don't tell me money doesn't buy happiness. Give me some money and let me find out for myself.

Politics – ask
no questions and
hear no spin.

Don't count
your chickens
until they've been
vaccinated against
Bird Flu.

Stop seizing the
day. Let someone
else have it for a
change.

Life is sweet:
brush your teeth
after every
incarnation.

Go green and save energy – stop mowing the lawn.

Don't cross your bridges till you know why there's heavy traffic coming the other way.

When you callously
end affairs, don't
assume all the
repercussions will
remain one-sided:
your lover's partner
will be scarred
for life, too.

If you enjoy an open marriage, don't be afraid to go to extremes. Try dating single people, just for a change.

Maybe you think the overweight don't try hard enough, but every day in every way they're getting butter and batter.

Unclutter your life – just buy a really big house.

Reduce your stress by learning to breathe slowly. Increase others' stress by practising on the telephone.

Learn to meditate
by taking time to
observe your
thoughts –
especially the
ones in bikinis.

Do everything in moderation: that includes doing everything in moderation.

When next you're dismayed by rain, consider that it falls on the righteous and sinful alike, but it also falls on women's t-shirts.

Keep a record of all
the bad things
you've ever done.
Make up some more
and add them. Sell it
to a newspaper.
Do bad things on
the proceeds till they
run out. Repeat.

Strive for Excellence rather than Perfection – it's worth more in Scrabble.

Take a different route to work – it will ruin your stalker's day.

Challenges
are wonderful
opportunities
to look at Life
differently: try
standing on one
leg and squinting.

If clouds really had silver linings they wouldn't float.

Did you hear about the prodigal cigarette manufacturer? He was led ashtray.

Two men looked
out of prison bars;
The first saw mud
and the second stars.
The second stood on
the head of the first;
The first must have
been concussed.

Do you own a boat? Does it have a large stern and move around aimlessly? Are you confident it won't go down? Then why not name it after your wife?

Is there someone
you love but
you're just no
good at giving
compliments?
Why not say
something hurtful
instead?

Only small people insist size doesn't matter.

Give Europeans 39 inches and they'll take a metre.

Incompatibility occurs when your spirit is willing but her flesh is repulsed.

Carpenters – many are called but few are affordable.

Always look both
ways when you
cross the road –
up and down.

Blessed are the poor
for they are least
likely to buy their
way out of poverty.

A trainee juggler
and his skittles are
soon parted.

Empty vessels make
the most television
appearances.

A bird may
defecate on a snake
but a snake would
be hard pushed to
respond in kind.

Do a brand new thing and they'll have to create a new crime to describe it.

WISDOM

OF LIFE

Good manners cost nothing. Cable not so.

At first I wept because I had no shoes. Then I met a man who had no feet; he didn't have any shoes for me, either.

'Come to the edge,' he said. 'We are afraid,' they said. But they came to the edge and he pushed them. And they sank like stones.

History tells us that pigs played a special part in the lives of the Celts and were attributed with the power of prophecy. Also, they were quite nice to eat.

Many a revolutionary thinker has turned the philosophical world on its head just to empty the coins from its pockets.

Piggy-eyed, short, fat, bald man, tends to sweat profusely, 35, unemployed, still a virgin, seeks unbelievably dumb blonde.

Soul-mate wanted.
No DSS or pets.

What the
caterpillar calls the
end of the world,
the master calls a
clumsy foot.

Red sky at night – a building's alight. Red sky at morning – it must have been highly flammable.

Judge not, lest ye have a newspaper column.

Dolphins murder fish. Moral: smiling makes everything acceptable.

The man with
a large shovel
will always be
welcome at the
Elephant House.

Pet a friendly dog
or cat but never on
the first date.

Have goals for
yourself. Then a
football pitch.
Pretty soon you'll
have your own
team.

Stretch your limits
a little each day;
we all need saggy
limits.

Know your limitations and let others know them too, by consistently failing.

Try putting air freshener in your car and then shit in the boot. After that it's a straight contest.

Remember
you always have
options, including
not remembering
that.

The planet spins through space at thousands of miles per hour. At that sort of speed, accidents are inevitable.

Practise non-
resistance but
don't be surprised
if you routinely
end up at the back
of the queue.

Treat a bad relationship as a learning opportunity – why not learn how to keep your partner faithful?

Every dog has its day – it's July 26th, National Dog Day.

Necessity is the
mother of invention
but servitude is
a bastard.

Every day in every
way I'm becoming
less self-centred.

Like father
like son but with
less money and
more hair.

THE LITTLE BOOK OF

FAILURE

MARC BLAKE

ISBN 1-905102-76-3, £2.99

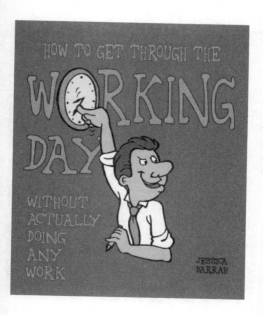

ISBN 1-905102-65-8, £2.99

ISBN 1-905102-59-3, £2.99

ARE YA' BOVVEREd?

500 REASONS NOt tO GIVE A SHIt

LEE BOK

ISBN 1-905102-75-5, £2.99

www.crombiejardine.com